WIT *and* WISDOM

Journeys through Career Transition

I0478576

Linda Lojewski and MaryAnne Sarzynski

WIT AND WISDOM
JOURNEYS THROUGH CAREER TRANSITION

iUniverse books may be ordered through booksellers or by contacting:

iUniverse
1663 Liberty Drive
Bloomington, IN 47403
www.iuniverse.com
1-800-Authors (1-800-288-4677)

Because of the dynamic nature of the Internet, any web addresses or
links contained in this book may have changed since publication and
may no longer be valid. The views expressed in this work are solely those
of the author and do not necessarily reflect the views of the publisher,
and the publisher hereby disclaims any responsibility for them.

Any people depicted in stock imagery provided by Thinkstock are models,
and such images are being used for illustrative purposes only.
Certain stock imagery © Thinkstock.

ISBN: 978-1-4917-7298-0 (sc)
ISBN: 978-1-4917-7299-7 (e)

Library of Congress Control Number: 2015911524

Print information available on the last page.

iUniverse rev. date: 12/17/2015

CONTENTS

Note: The journeys reflect the point in time in which the interviews were conducted.

ACKNOWLEDGEMENTS

This book was made possible thanks to many contributors. This includes the women who shared their journeys and others who offered advice, resources and support. Special thanks to Alma Azua-Cassady, Mary Bowler, Helen Cooke, Dr. Glenna Crooks, Deb Dellapena, Monica Heuer, Cindy Murray and Charlotte Sibley.

CHARLOTTE SIBLEY...
Charlotte Sibley, pharmaceutical executive and 2008 Healthcare Businesswomen's Association (HBA) Woman of the Year

Charlotte's Transition Tip:

"When you find yourself in career transition, put your energy into something outside yourself: Volunteer! It gives you a different perspective, you do real work, you get validation, you gain additional expertise... and the networking is great."

MARY BOWLER...

Mary E. Bowler, President of Bowler and Company Consulting, LLC

Mary's Transition Tip:

"We are successful, accomplished women and have impacted the lives of many – inside and outside of the workplace. This success does not end when one is in transition. Stand tall, smile, and carry that success with you into each and every meeting and enjoy the opportunity for a new beginning."

INTRODUCTION

In 2009, a handful of professional women in suburban Philadelphia, who had been displaced by their employers, appreciated the scale of corporate downsizing in the region. They formed a group to help others in career transition. Although it had been the hope of the group's founders that the need would be brief, more than six years later the group persists.

Started by women who belonged to the same professional organization for healthcare businesswomen, the group members had a collegial relationship. They came to be known as WIT (Women In Transition) led by a series of women who have contributed their skills and talents for the benefit of those in transition, as well as for other leaders to follow.

WIT is an amazing group of successful women who shared contacts, support, knowledge and good humor. Membership openness and authenticity created a unique and effective dynamic.

These women served as the inspiration for this book. This was reinforced listening to each woman tell her story about how the failing economy and the transforming industry impacted her personally. These interviews show how these women nimbly responded to the changing employment environment.

This collection of career transition journeys is intended to offer the resolve, humor, generosity, and wisdom of women who are leaders sharing their insights and talents for the benefit of others in the spirit of legacy. The messages in this book are valuable whether or not a person is in active job search. At some point within the span of any career, transitions inevitability will occur.

Some transitions are planned others are not. There are many useful tips offered by those who have contributed to this book, including suggestions for steps that may be taken while employed to support smooth and productive career transitions.

Enjoy!

THE WOMEN OF WIT AND THEIR JOURNEYS

ROBYN V. ALLEN-MCKINNON, MPH, MBA
Life Sciences Commercial Operations,
Proven Market Access & Financial Leader

Consistently strong performance may not spare you from downsizing but can help you to find your next opportunity.

After a larger drug manufacturer acquired her company, Robyn Allen-McKinnon learned there would be job cuts. Because performance had been a consideration, Robyn felt reassured. Robyn's sense of reassurance proved premature – because, while her performance was consistently strong, it was just one factor in the decision-making. Eventually, Robyn was involuntarily terminated.

Since her school days, Robyn had added a wealth of experience to her resume. She worked steadily to develop and refine her skills at major companies like Abbott, Hospira and Wyeth. Over time, her performance reviews and recognition gave shape to a compendium of accomplishments and served as evidence of her mastery of her discipline. With her extensive practical experience and education (an undergraduate degree from Cornell, and graduate degrees from Columbia University and the University of Virginia), Robyn felt well equipped for a relatively quick job search.

Determined to find a job close to home within three months, she viewed her severance package as a windfall. She stashed it into savings for her children's college educations.

Because Robyn's focus remained more on her job than her career during the turbulent environment within her company, she didn't fully appreciate the impact of the pharmaceutical industry's contraction within her target region. She knew drug manufacturers everywhere were steadily shedding thousands of employees. However, like so many others, Robyn's past job search experience misinformed her present point of view.

Upon initiating her job search, Robyn recognized thousands of others like her: established, well-educated, and experienced professionals. She also shared with many the added complexities of having children in school and spouses locally employed. It was especially competitive in the Delaware Valley area of the mid-Atlantic region Robyn pursued.

Ultimately her job search spanned 17 months. Her severance and unemployment compensation became necessary for living expenses. Toward the end of her job search, money she'd saved for her children's educations was exhausted.

Prepare.

Here are a few tips to prepare:
- Consider best and worst case scenarios
- Identify factors that signal which case is playing out
- Be ready to recalibrate

Eventually, Robyn recalibrated the geographic range of her search. "Because my search time increased from a few months to more than a year, I expanded it beyond big pharma companies close to home. I included small and mid-size companies and non-profit organizations. My commute threshold increased to a 90-minute drive," she says.

Despite a great support system, an extended job search challenged her self-confidence. The longer it continued, the less it seemed likely she would land a role at her former director level. Despite knowing she wasn't alone, she found the bi-weekly, unemployment compensation process, especially difficult.

Her typically positive attitude suffered. Her family told her she was becoming moody. "My personality changed and I became depressed... I was increasingly cynical in my thinking," she recalls, "I am a spiritual person, so I kept asking God why I lost my job, what lesson I needed to learn. I persevered."

Volunteering is important.

Volunteering gives you the opportunity to share your talents with others, allows you to showcase your skills and provides you the opportunity to experiment, grow and lead.

One of her colleagues recommended an industry support group for women in career transition. Like her, they were highly educated, experienced and successful women in the same situation.

Seeing an opportunity to contribute, Robyn volunteered to assist in adding infrastructure and collaborative tools to the networking group. She helped co-create and implement processes for information storage, sharing and tracking group activities. Using digital technologies, the team extended the organization's value from bi-weekly, face-to-face meetings to an on-demand hub for 24/7 access to communications and resources.

Get out of your comfort zone.

Prior to her job loss, Robyn was not much of a networker. Transition forced her to step out of her comfort zone. She started going to networking functions and soon she met other dynamic people, developed professional relationships and friendships.

Today, Robyn believes in the value of networking. It strengthened her confidence and reinforced her value in the marketplace. In addition, she took project management classes and provided financial management guidance to entrepreneurs. These endeavors helped enrich her resume, as well as renew her spirit.

Know the marketplace and get realistic about your goals.

"Ultimately, I accepted a position at a level below my former role at a company an hour's drive from my home. I am grateful to have it," she says. "I am doing financial analysis and planning within the pharmaceutical industry - work I did a decade ago." Getting realistic about goals means being flexible and willing to adjust expectations.

Transition taught her to see herself and the world in a different view. It empowered Robyn to connect and explore opportunities, ultimately helping her grow.

Photo: Robyn enjoys family time
at the Port of Philadelphia.

ALMA AZUA-CASSADY
Global Marketer Fluent in Three Languages

Planning is time-consuming, but worth the effort.

Planning takes time but thinking ahead will inform your actions and decision-making. It helps you move forward in a focused and efficient manner. For Alma, the first six months of career transition were focused on planning her job search strategy. This included defining her personal brand and her position in the marketplace.

As an award-winning marketer, fluent in English, Spanish and French, Alma knew she had a unique skillset. This skillset would differentiate her "brand" in competition for the global marketing roles she wanted. She also targeted employers and roles that matched her level of experience.

The right job search strategy is the one that is best for you.

Your search strategy may be quite different from that of your peers. That's okay. To identify your best strategy, be clear and specific about your near-term and long-term goals and what defines success for you.

For Alma, once the planning groundwork was complete, she executed her job search strategy by establishing a broader network to connect with target employers. This takes work because even with the best plans, it's not easy to convert informational meetings and job leads into interviews.

Determine how you will assess the effectiveness of your strategy.

If you were a high earner, the job search could take a year or more. Define the indicators that will inform whether or not you are getting closer to your goal.

When it began to take longer than Alma expected to yield results, she re-adjusted her expectations. She consulted part-time, sought speaking engagements, and volunteered at professional organizations. This increased her visibility and showcased her strengths. It also provided needed income during the job search.

Diversify your skills.

Consulting and contracting roles can offer many opportunities in transition. You can expand your breadth of experience and explore ways to transfer your skills to other functions and industries. Alma recommends being ready and willing to look outside of your present industry to adjacent businesses. For instance, roles with healthcare insurers and hospital networks offer opportunity and can broaden professional experience.

ROBBYN BHATT, MBA
Marketing and Business Development Expert

Regain your footing by seizing the opportunities that the disruption may offer.

When your career has been a succession of roles with increasing responsibility, you have evidence you're proficient in your discipline. You've demonstrated your ability to focus and control your professional universe in order to achieve business objectives. Transition is disruptive. "It creates a sense of being out of control of your universe and this can be destabilizing," says Robbyn.

For some, transition disrupts the sense of control they feel over their own world. One way to regain a sense of control is to seize the opportunities transition can bring. Do things for personal renewal.

In Robbyn's case, spoiling herself was as simple as: sleeping a little later some mornings, walking the dog, finishing a book, and investing in new and old friendships. She visited her sister, joined her husband on business trips and re-connected with colleagues and friends.

Add a human touch by thinking outside the house.

Because Robbyn had experienced transition in the past, she knew what to expect: a rollercoaster, with both good and bad weeks. A good week may be email responses from prospective employers. A bad week may be simply feeling transition will never end.

In the digital era, resumes are submitted electronically. They are keyword-searched by computers to screen candidates. Then, computers issue letters to advise applicants whether a resume has been rejected or has advanced in the system. This impersonal phase of the job search can be especially lonely in its early phase. This may mean "thinking out of the house."

To reduce the silence of job search hours at her computer, Robbyn and a friend alternated meeting at each other's homes to search together. It became a pleasant social outlet as well as mutual support and exchange of ideas during the process.

Many people work at cafes with free-WIFI, which serve as an informal co-working situation.

Start your week on a positive note.

At WIT, attendees share useful information in a safe environment. The group, founded by women in career transition, meet bi-weekly on Monday mornings. Robbyn says, "It was a social outlet that offered support and friendly faces. It reminds you you're not alone."

Transition can give way to self-awareness and personal growth.

The biggest surprise during Robbyn's transition was the personal growth and understanding she realized. "Being in transition offers time to think about how you got to this point in your life and how it makes you feel," says Robbyn. There is time to reflect upon what is important to you. This includes what work really means to you. Did it represent too big a part of your identity? Was your sense of self-worth primarily derived from your role as a professional and, now, with that gone, has your worth somehow diminished? According to Robbyn, transition uncovers these questions and makes you think about your life in a new way.

Work experience is part of social network and self-worth.

Robbyn says there are elements of the work experience that allow you to get comfortable in a routine. There is the social network of relationships that evolve over time and reinforce work experience as your identity.

To help her expand and redevelop her identity, Robbyn took classes at community colleges, the local hospital and via Coursera, a massive open online course (MOOC). MOOCs are free and offer certificates of completion for doing required work. She also volunteered at Cradles to Crayons.

These activities enriched her personally and helped expand her network beyond the pharmaceuticals industry. Perhaps, most importantly, she found she liked volunteerism; it helped her discover and acknowledge other aspects of herself.

Act with positive energy to yield positive results.

At a professional networking meeting, Robbyn suggested the group plan a future program focused on how to start a non-profit. Like others in career transition, she had been doing more volunteer work. Robbyn wanted to learn more about the non-profit world and thought others would be interested as well.

Robbyn reached out to a founder of a non-profit who eagerly accepted the invitation. A few weeks later he presented to nearly a dozen attendees. Although none of the attendees chose to start their own non-profit, Robbyn's suggestion motivated volunteers and helped dozens of young people.

What is in a title?

Don't allow a job title to stand between you and progress. Sure, it's tough on the ego to accept a job with a lesser title and responsibilities. However, if the supply of superb candidates is greater than the demand, your dilemma is a simple math equation.

Early in her job search, Robbyn sought to parlay her industry knowledge into new fields like e-prescribing and electronic medical records. At that time, her search revealed that the electronic tools in healthcare were still developing and in the technical phase, not ready for downstream marketing, so she broadened her search beyond the pharmaceutical industry. This allowed her to explore more opportunities and fully tap into her skills and make a contribution.

The economy influenced her expectations for her next job. She knows she's smart and has proven her skills over time, but also understood reality. The troubled economy was less likely to produce more jobs paying the salaries of the recent past - particularly within the Greater Philadelphia area.

She remains optimistic the economy will improve and she'll have the opportunity to move up through the ranks to increase her salary. However, throughout her search, Robbyn was determined to find an employer that was staffed with smart, good people who believed in their work and were committed. Her search became more focused on job satisfaction than a paycheck.

Networking Yields Opportunity

Robbyn accepted a bridge role, a part-time, contract position within a discipline she really enjoyed. Subsequently Robbyn moved into other roles within healthcare and enhanced her expertise. As of this writing she accepted a position with Horizon Health Services.

While another transition is possible, she knows she has a valuable knowledge base and experience working in a variety of corporate cultures. She demonstrated her ability to adapt and flourish through change.

THE FLEXPRO GROUP...

Website: http://www.theflexprogroup.com

Delivering Project Management Expertise to Companies in the Life Sciences

Recognized by *Inc. Magazine* as one of America's fastest-growing private companies: #859 (2014), #288 (2013) and #104 (2012).

Ranked 6th on the Philadelphia 100 list of fastest growing privately held companies (2013 and 2012).

In 2008, Rose Cook and her identical twin-sister, Lynn Faughey, founded The FlexPro Group, a specialty-consulting firm delivering project management expertise to companies in the life sciences.

The company's areas of focus include: Research and Development, Supply Chain Operations, and Project Management Systems. Clients are progressive industry leaders who look to The FlexPro Group as a strategic partner helping them achieve smart solutions.

Both Rose and Lynn had successful careers when they formed The FlexPro Group. After starting their families, they wanted more work / life flexibility and balance. FlexPro's consulting roles are well-suited for challenging, yet flexible work opportunities. Clients benefit from the specialized expertise of the consultants and their ability to "hit the ground running."

The Outsourcing Evolution

The outsourcing trend began with mailrooms and call centers, then maintenance and food services groups. In its early days, outsourcing led to the growth of companies like Aramark who took over food services operations for schools, corporations and sports arenas. In theory, outsourcing companies bring efficiency and cost reductions. However, in its early days, cost-cutting often resulted in reduced quality service. With customer dissatisfaction came customer defections. The cost to acquire and retain customers soon outweighed the savings.

The demand for higher quality and operational cost reductions paralleled technological advances. Technology helped many industries successfully improve the customer experience, thus increasing customer retention. In recent years, outsourcing has expanded to professional services, including consulting for project management, supply chain, compliance, finance, legal, and human resources.

The trend is expected to continue leading to a veritable boom for The FlexPro Group and other outsourcing companies. Labor statistics support this assertion, The Bureau of Labor Statistics January 2012 Monthly Labor Review indicated,

"Employment in professional and business services is projected to add 3.8 million jobs (second largest among all major sectors), to reach 20.5 million in 2020. The management, scientific, and technical consulting services industry is responsible for the majority of the employment growth in professional and business services. Employment is projected to increase by 575,600 jobs, or 4.7 percent annually, reaching a level of 1.6 million by 2020. This industry is expected to have one of the largest and fastest employment increases of all industries. Businesses' increasing use of consulting services to keep pace with the latest technologies, government regulations, and management and production techniques will increase the demand for workers in the industry.

Services of consultants can be a lower cost alternative, because consultants can be hired temporarily and as needed. Real output in the management, scientific, and technical consulting services industry is projected to rise by $76.1 billion, a 3.8-percent annual increase, to reach $242.9 billion by 2020."

Embrace the New Reality

The relatively recent, but inevitable, action of the pharmaceuticals industry has acutely impacted the greater Philadelphia region. Thousands of highly skilled people have found themselves jobless, often after decades of service. However, challenging times bring opportunities.

Rose Cook encourages job seekers to consider the advantages of being a contracted consultant. "It's not for everyone. If you don't like change, you won't enjoy consulting," says Rose. "As a contracted consultant, you have the opportunity to work in different environments that offer diversity of experience – something that wouldn't be possible in the traditional corporate environment."

Companies are smarter about how they work and use their resources. These shifts include technological advances and a work-force eligible population that spans five generations. Rather than taking time and money to hire and develop employees in specific areas of expertise, companies are hiring consultants who have that experience and expertise and can deliver it on demand. With advances in technology emerging from smaller businesses, Rose expects her pool of experts to be sustainable even after the pool of post big-pharma experts dwindles in a decade or so.

Rose notes that larger companies will still need core directors to set strategy and chart the course toward achievement of business goals. However, going forward, corporate directors will be managing contracted teams in addition to people employed directly by their companies.

Expand Your Skillset, Grow Expertise

Contracted employees often have experience working at more than one large company giving them exposure to varying corporate cultures. The emotional intelligence that people develop over time from experience in varying work settings is invaluable. Experience helps contracted consultants quickly and effectively integrate into new organizations. The most successful contracted employees have the ability to adapt to the work environment they land in.

Key traits for success:

- experience working in different corporate cultures
- ability to adapt quickly in new environments *(often more important than knowledge base)*
- enjoy variety in work tasks and willingness to try new work tasks
- ability to navigate complex, matrix work environments with low need for supervision

Key gains:

- exposure to new areas
- opportunity to develop new skills sets *(not always feasible in a traditional work setting)*
- flexibility that can enhance work / life balance
- opportunity to increase professional network

Keep in mind:

- accept you don't "own" the project; you might not be part of the final project.
- understand that it's okay that you are not "part of a company's family" and may not be included in group lunches or celebrations. It's not personal.
- enjoy the variety of each project and seize opportunities to broaden your skills set

ROSE COOK
CEO and Co-Founder, The FlexPro Group,
SmartCEO's Philadelphia Brava! Award July 2014
Inc. Magazine's Top Female CEO and Top Asian
Entrepreneur

Transition to CEO

Rose began her career in 1988 as a packaging machinery engineer at Nabisco after graduating from Rutgers University with a B.S. in mechanical engineering. Within a year, she moved to Johnson & Johnson's Ortho-McNeil company as a packaging supervisor. From there she went to Colgate Palmolive for one year, eventually returning to Johnson & Johnson's pharmaceutical sourcing group.

The J&J culture made it clear the quickest way to get ahead was to "punch your card." In that spirit, Rose worked hard acquiring an in-depth and varied range of expertise. In 2001, she left J&J and formed Rose Cook Associates. Her company provided project management services exclusively to J&J.

In a relatively short time, Rose chose to take down her shingle and returned to J&J. Three years later, she was promoted to Director of Packaging

Engineering. Looking for greater autonomy to balance work, family and other obligations, in 2008, she took the leap and formed The FlexPro Group and hasn't looked back.

LYNN FAUGHEY
Chief Operating Officer and Co-Founder, The FlexPro Group

Transition to Entrepreneur

Lynn started her career as a global packaging engineer at Colgate-Palmolive in 1988 after graduating from Rutgers University. By 1991, Lynn had accepted a position with Johnson & Johnson as a packaging engineer at McNeil Consumer Products. During her time there, she held various positions of increasing responsibility including packaging and commodities manager for the J&J / Merck consumer products partnership.

Later she switched gears and started a decorating consultant business called Decorating 101 from 2002 to 2005. In 2005, she changed course again and returned to J&J as a consultant, which led to re-joining J&J full-time as a project manager until she later partnered with her sister, Rose, to form The FlexPro Group.

TERESA FANTACONE
Corporate Communications Strategist

Be career-centric

Being career-centric rather than job focused can help you achieve the level of success and longevity you seek professionally. Nurture your network before, during and after career transition. Odds are your next job will come from a lead acquired through your network.

With expertise in Corporate Communications and Public Affairs, Teresa was already adept at identifying stakeholders, developing rapport and building collaborations to achieve goals. Therefore, she readily applied those skills to her time in transition and vigorously re-engaged in networking. She became active in organizations such as HBA (Healthcare Businesswomen's Association), HBA sub-group Women in Transition (WIT) and Greater Philadelphia Senior Executives Group, (GPSEG).

In addition to getting up-to-speed with networking, Teresa needed to learn more about technology in the job search. It significantly changed the transition experience. Fortunately groups such as WIT and a contracted outplacement center (a benefit of her severance package) helped with the electronic job application process, resume development, use of key words, and a social media strategy.

Teresa always appreciated the value of a strong network, however, the demands of her job always took priority. Therefore, the time in transition proved valuable for re-establishing and nurturing her network. Teresa's experience with GPSEG was especially productive because it helped expand her network beyond the pharmaceutical industry.

A key insight from Teresa is the passion and commitment to a job should be balanced with passion and commitment for your own professional growth.

Take time to do what you love!

It may seem counter-intuitive, but during transition you need to do things you enjoy.

Volunteer! Take a class. Ride a bike. Doing what you love will give you the emotional energy you need, especially during a pro-longed job search. This helps you exude positive energy on interviews.

In addition to developing her "for profit" network, Teresa pursued non-profit interests and increased her volunteerism. She volunteers at the Main Line Animal Rescue and helps puppy mill and abused dogs build their self-confidence. She also kept her skills sharp by creating social media content for a Philadelphia non-profit called, "Back on My Feet." Through this non-profit channel, Teresa learned about non-profit leadership training, so she took classes to learn about running a non-profit and fundraising.

Career transition is a time to get out of your comfort zone.

A good first step is to identify the growth businesses within your target geography and locate job opportunities seeking your skillsets. When planning a job search strategy, face the realities of the market and the demand for your skills. If your search efforts are not yielding results, ask yourself some hard questions:

- Where is the true demand for my skills and experience?

- Who, what and where is my competition?
- How am I differentiating my skills and experience relative to the competition? Do I have a competitive advantage?
- What is the marketplace value for my skills and experience? Has it changed? Do my expectations match that change?

With so many mid-to-senior level pharmaceutical professionals in transition, the marketplace was extremely competitive for jobs in that industry. Teresa resisted the impulse to focus on a familiar industry. She researched other area businesses. Teresa suggests investigating growth industries across different sectors and in-demand roles to explore and discover how your skills can transfer.

Know yourself and know where you can be flexible.

Teresa loves the Greater Philadelphia area. She rehabbed her home and now it "fits like a slipper." With family local and four dogs, she was not interested in relocating. But she did slightly widened her search geography and found it offered more opportunities. The key to making the most of your time in transition is to plan ahead and use it strategically.

Photo: Teresa with her pets at holiday time.

JANE FAYER, MBA
Consultant at Fayer Associates, LLC

Clinical Outsourcing and Alliance Management

Hey, this is different than I expected.

When Jane learned her job had been eliminated, she was shocked. Always a good performer and a hard worker, regularly working 10-to-12-hour days, accessible 24/7, she knew the company was downsizing, but she didn't expect it to happen to her. After all, most professionals were used to being aggressively recruited for well-paying jobs throughout their careers. Being downsized hit hard - especially when she wasn't offered an alternative position. Jane thought her commitment and dedication would extend to her retirement, instead her role was off-shored to India. Jane was unemployed.

The experience left Jane feeling burned out. It was months before she could tell people she lost her job. "It was painful and personal." It seemed to her that the company had based its decisions to re-size and sub-contract on short-term and shortsighted pandering to Wall Street. Jane likened the company's actions and direction to a scene from the Star Trek Borg movie where one character stated, "you will be assimilated." She had no choice but to accept what happened and move on.

She gave herself two weeks to recoup before looking for a job. Two weeks turned into two months. She had no idea how hard it could be for well-educated and experienced people to find jobs.

You don't always manifest what you envision. Sometimes your life plan is unexpectedly disrupted by factors beyond your control. After the shock, do some reflection for insight regarding cues you may have missed. Then, accept and move on.

Moving On… Discovering WIT… Establishing CIT

Jane belonged to the Metro Chapter of the professional organization HBA. When a nearby Chapter planned a five-year celebration, Jane attended. There she met Sue Price, co-chair of WIT, and discovered the Greater Philadelphia region had a subgroup to support women in transition.

At that time, WIT was meeting regularly in King of Prussia, Pennsylvania, Jane went to her first meeting and found a welcoming group who made her feel comfortable. Jane became a regular at WIT meetings, joined the Greater Philadelphia Chapter of HBA, and soon became a WIT co-chair herself.

When Jane connected with Cathy Pariser, an HBA Metro Chapter member, they reached out to the HBA Metro group to form a career transition group.

Jane noticed a few things while in transition:

- Her employed colleagues didn't fully appreciate the seismic shift in the marketplace
- She understood how strongly she had defined herself in terms of her professional life
- Separation from work meant Jane's life was drastically altered
- Everyone else was getting up and going to work; she had nowhere to go in the morning

This left her feeling fearful, sad and anxious. Jane feared the worst, which is common during major life changes, she wouldn't find another job and would have to move in with relatives due to financial constraints. This type of extreme and perhaps unwarranted concern is common in people when huge, unexpected changes occur.

From anxiety and fear to joy and purpose...

Jane attended an HBA program at St. Joseph's University and the speaker asked, "What would you do if money was not a consideration? What would you do with your life?" Answering this question would ultimately change her life.

"It was a life changing moment for me," says Jane, "I was interested in art and wanted to do something with art my entire life, but I had never had the time," says Jane.

She began volunteering at the Barnes Foundation, founded in 1922 by Albert C. Barnes, a chemist who collected art after profiting from by co-developing the drug marketed as Argyrol.

The foundation has thousands of art objects and approximately 800 impressionist and modernist paintings worth billions. This creative environment reinvigorated Jane.

Jane's Barnes experience, created a more multidimensional life experience for her, offering balance. "I am living my dreams," she says. "I will never feel worthless due to a job loss again."

Tap into your inner entrepreneur!

At the same time Jane began volunteering at the Barnes Foundation, she began contract work as a bridge to consulting. She found a contracting job online at Indeed.com doing something she'd never done before: alliance management. Soon after, she realized the company's environment was not a good match. "It was empowering to choose my work environment!" Later she started doing independent consulting (self-employed, collecting payment for work via IRS 1099-Miscellaneous Income Form) and worked on her terms.

Transition changed her personally and professionally. She no longer views a future role as permanent. She's enjoying the work / life balance consulting offers.

KAREN FRIEDMAN

Chief Improvement Officer at Karen Friendman Enterprises, Entrepreneur, Communications Coach, Best-Selling Author, Columnist, Media & Presentations Trainer, Crisis Manager, Speaker

As the Workplace Changes, Change with It

The workplace has changed across the board and individuals have to evolve with it. No longer is there a clear right or wrong career path. For some, adapting to the environment may mean becoming an entrepreneur or translating skills into new roles. Going out on your own is not for everyone. Karen suggests that what seems daunting can be doable and transition may give you time to reinvent yourself.

For 20 years Karen Friedman was a television reporter and loved it. As TV news outlets were expanding, reporters were required to be live in the field and be on-call to report early morning fires or late at night to cover gunshot wounds at bars – time away from her two small children at home. It was time to move on. After 12 years at ABC in Philly, Karen was ready for new challenges but not sure where.

She knew her strengths; getting people to open up and that she could think on her feet, but it wasn't obvious how these could translate into a new job. In time, she figured out how to translate her skills in the workplace to skills that could help others succeed.

When Karen started her own business more than 18 years ago, she offered mostly media and crisis training and message development. She helped executives fine-tune their message and get to the point quickly. Karen expanded her business to include leadership communication, speaker and presentation training, along with opinion leader coaching. Wyeth Pharmaceuticals was one of her first clients.

Karen's Transition Tips:

- Ask others what they really value about you. You'll realize how others see you and how to leverage those skills as a job. "We all have our own unique strengths," says Karen. "In my programs, I challenge women to ask: What am I good at? What makes me different, unique? How do I want others to describe me?"

- Sometimes people like their company but want to change their role. Karen calls it going through transition while employed. The process is the same, you have to ask: "How can I bring my skills to a different division?" One of Karen's colleagues worked in pharma but wanted something else. She found a new role where she helped others more directly - in patient advocacy

- Because the workplace is constantly evolving, learning to proactively convert skills and talents so that they remain aligned with marketplace demand is essential. Soft and hard skills need to be looked at and re-evaluated.

- Ask yourself, "What do I love doing versus what sucks the energy out of me and makes me want to stay in bed all day?" Karen recalls the story of a woman she met who wanted to act and sing on Broadway. She gave herself 5 years to try. Ten years later she was still doing the same thing, some acting and waiting on tables. Today, she is a professional speaker, who found a way to merge her singing/song writing with her presentations by regularly mixing speaking themes and songs she's written about the topics. This person is living her passion.

Times of transition can be a journey of self-discovery.

Knowing our strengths and sources of energy is important. For example, Karen's husband worked in marketing and sales in technology. While he was in transition, he started a business doing what he loves - furniture construction. He discovered he didn't enjoy it as a business because the activity shifted from a creative outlet to work.

"I spent my whole career on live television," says Karen, "I'm still in front of audiences and I get charged that way." Karen's company helps people from all industries and from countries around the world to be more effective and compelling communicators, offering individual coaching, small and large group programs, speeches at seminars, training, and patient and advocacy story-telling programs. For pharma clients, Karen takes complicated information and data and makes it accessible and interesting. "The core communications principles apply regardless of the medium," she says.

When you identify your core strengths, you're ready to explore how to translate your talents into your next career. Get Karen's video tips and her book, *"Shut Up and Say Something"* at: http://www.karenfriedman.com

MAUREEN HALL

Award-Winning Digital Marketer, Founder & CEO of Digital Marketing Agency, Past HBA Board Member

Career transition from service-side to client-side

Maureen Hall likes to see how the fit pieces fit together. That's why a favorite stress-reliever is doing crossword puzzles.

Throughout her career as a social media and digital healthcare marketing strategist, she's been adept at putting the right pieces together in business - she has the accolades and awards to prove it. As Founder and CEO of Hall Media Productions, Maureen repeatedly demonstrated skill in assembling a strong team and then selling the expertise required to acquire work. "It is fun to work with clients and a good team," she says.

Using the persona "Maureen Hall: Media Maven (Views from the Cloud)," she became a recognized opinion leader in health care on the use of digital media. She's passionate about using technology to enable improved health and wellness behaviors and specializes in connecting patients with actionable information, helping them to choose better paths. Maureen's vision is to use her talents and experience to make the world a healthier place.

Apply marketing principles to the job search.

Maureen's two-year transition began when she sold Hall Media Productions, the company she founded in 1995. She looked forward to the change, but it came with challenges. When she sold her company she also sold her "branding." While the process to establish product branding and positioning is energizing for marketers, the process can be daunting when the product is you.

To add to this major identity change, she hadn't written a resume in nearly 30 years and she did not complete her degree at the University of Pennsylvania, where she went to college.

Maureen's Challenges

- She knew having a degree was critical to make it through the digital screening
- Her highly valued soft skills - essential for business leaders - are a challenge to feature when applying online

Maureen's Solutions

- She created a list of target companies and met prospective hiring managers.
- She knew a positive rapport with her employer was essential to achieve to her patient-focused objectives.
- Maureen engaged in networking groups while developing her personal brand and resume. She transitioned from the project work she was doing to kick-off her next career search.
- She volunteered as a digital and social mentor for start-up companies at the *University Science Center Incubator, a gathering place for new ideas, creative exchange and development of products and technology in Philadelphia. This helped spotlight her skills.

*For professionals, investors, and academics-- The University Science Center Incubator (http://www.sciencecenter.org) has many year-around educational and networking event opportunities.

Remain committed to your plan.

After years on the agency side, Maureen knew she wanted to "own the product" and drive its success. Her forward thinking told her the industry was at a nexus where technology and the environment were ready for the catalyst to connect people with brands in innovative ways. Maureen wanted to be that catalyst and it was the driving force throughout her job search.

Remaining true to her plan, she landed a position in need of her vast experience and skills to connect people with healthcare resources for improved outcomes. As Digital Marketing Leader for Vree Health, a subsidiary of Merck focused on technology-enabled services to improve healthcare through better connections. She's the catalyst for positive healthcare change she envisioned.

Photo: Maureen Backpacking
at the Grand Canyon

Photo: Maureen on a bike ride

KATE HERMANS
Global Brand Development & Commercialization

Time for reflection of personal and professional priorities.

For Kate Hermans, former General Manager for a pharmaceutical business unit in China, the transition experience was wonderful, she decompressed after more than 20 years of non-stop work. Transition provided time to reflect on what was important personally and professionally and it brought clarity, allowing her to focus on what she wanted to do next.

Networking is "people helping people."

She met new people and reconnected with acquaintances. "I was touched by the advice and support I received, by the sheer generosity of people willing to help," says Kate. She was reminded that networking is "people helping people." "Everyone should be networking for life."

Think strategically about network groups. A longer-term commitment helps you to "pay it forward."

Kate joined networking and non-profit groups she would remain active with during and after transition.

Turn the transition journey into an empowering experience.

Initially transition arrived with a sense of "emptiness," but as Kate soul-searched about what she wanted to do, she was empowered by the freedom to be thoughtful and specific.

She enjoyed working as a consultant because she met new people and worked in areas of her expertise. It gave her exposure to a variety of organizations, kept her up-to-date with the marketplace, and gave her a sense of purpose - beyond looking for her next job. "There is a whole 'sub-culture' of people consulting either temporarily or permanently which offers another network to access."

The employer / employee contract: Know the terms. Know the changes for no surprises.

While interviewing for full-time positions, she found most companies are understanding of people in transition as long as they remained active and invested in their areas of expertise. "The industry is changing. Some companies will adapt. There are individuals who adapt and those who don't. An important lesson for me is the "contract" between the employer and the employee must be good for both," says Kate.

Kate found her type of role in a biopharmaceutical company. Thanks to her introspection and planning, she created the future she envisioned.

"Transition is change and change can be scary," says Kate, "unless you embrace it as an opportunity to shape your future." When Kate reflects upon her WIT experience, she notes that, "The support I received from WIT was enormously important. I am lucky to have found WIT and enjoy keeping in touch with the great women I met through the experience."

JENNIFER JASKOWIAK, BA, CHEMISTRY, MBA

Biotech / Pharma Product Development Expert, Committed to Achieving a Role in Patient Advocacy, Translating Science and Strategy into Action for Patients

Passion for patient advocacy led to a career shift.

Jennifer's career aspirations shifted after working on a rare-disease project. There are fewer patients with rare diseases; therefore, the opportunity to realize a meaningful impact in a more direct way is greater. There is a sense of connectedness and intimacy with the patient community and an opportunity to improve the quality of life and lifespan of patients.

Her professional development plan at work effectively defined her career on a narrow track within the company – not the personal growth track she aspired. She needed to find a way to realign her personal and professional ambitions. So, she created a personal development plan that defined goals and a strategy to align the personal and professional. Jennifer consulted with others and received positive feedback on her plans. With confidence that she could take her knowledge and expertise to the next level, Jennifer left her job to pursue the role of patient advocate.

Change can be...

Change can be both exhilarating and exasperating. While the prospect of charting a new career path can be invigorating, it's not without moments of fear and frustration. Jennifer had to address some challenging questions:

- How long do you allow yourself to make the career change?
- How do you cope with moments of discouragement and discomfort, especially when you no longer have your former income and benefits?
- What is your back-up plan? Do you just plan for success in the new track?

Committed to bringing healing technology to patients

Thanks to a carefully crafted plan for her next-career, Jennifer set in place a clear vision for her future. She chose a mix of options to keep her skills sharp, explore advocacy through startups, consulting, volunteering at Johns Hopkins University Graduate Student Social Entrepreneurship Program and in leadership for the HBA as the Vice President elect for the Mid-Atlantic Chapter. Jennifer also volunteered as a co-chair for WIT, bringing her skills and talents to further extend and evolve this very fluid and adaptive group so that it may continue to offer support to women in transition. Her passion, commitment and tenacity will no doubt transition her plan to a reality.

JULIA KELLY
Client Strategy, Sales, Marketing, Operations, and Business Development

Why did this happen to me?

When Julia was displaced from a major pharmaceutical company after 15 years, the thoughts that entered her mind were typical: "Why did they let me go? I worked so hard! I gave my blood! I am better/smarter/more valuable than Horton and Agnes!"

But as the reality of looking for a new position set in, Julia realized that job separation is similar to divorce. At first she was in shock and reluctant to take action, she later realized that moving on required hard work in the form of reflection, which helped prepare Julia for her search.

These are a few things to generally consider as you reflect on your previous job:

- What did and did not work?
- The job loss may have been out of your control
- There is hope for another role/relationship
- Prepare a succinct and positive explanation for the loss to use as you interview and network for your next opportunity

Stop Obsessing! Put your energy into your job search.

Once Julia reviewed and processed thoughts from her previous job, she understood that agonizing over it wasn't productive. Finding the best, new role required focused activity, so she shifted her thinking and developed a strategy with action items.

I will never ever find a job. Ever.

A big myth that can permeate your thoughts during job search is, "I will never find a job!" This is an illusion, best dissolved by taking control of your search. Create a search strategy, a plan and a timeline before you enter the market.

In February 2013, Julia joined WIT and attended the bi-weekly meetings. She went to other business networking events to build her network. By May 2013, Julia was HBA Woman of the Year (WOTY) Chair. This event is the largest HBA program of the year.

"At WOTY I sat next to Ken Frazier, CEO of Merck. What a fantastic opportunity to reach a wider audience," says Julia. by November 2013 she was added to the slate for the HBA Corporate Board of Directors. Her actions had provided amazing returns. She was networking and giving back through volunteering which Julia said was personally and professionally rejuvenating.

Julia's Tips:
- Invest in a professional resume writing service. This is a critical marketing tool.
- What roles or titles do I want to hold?
- What industries do I want to pursue?
- What are my geographic preferences?
- What are the target companies?
- What training do I need to fill my gaps?
- What amount of travel am I willing to accept?
- What are the critical elements of my compensation package?
- Invest in resources with a maximum return
- Be realistic and do not expect everyone to help you
- Take time to help others in transition

- Once you land a new role—give thought to your next move while you are still employed

Remember finding the new job may not meet your timeline. It may take a little longer, but you WILL FIND A JOB!

I'm not going to apply because I don't have ALL the job requirements.

"Horse hockey!" says Julia. "If you have most of the elements, apply. Why would you take a job where there is nothing to learn?" Be open to the possibilities. Be flexible.

"I am not _____ enough" and other self-deprecating thoughts.

Self-doubt is a natural reaction. Stop it! Julia advises, "Make a list of all your good traits, your accomplishments, your skills and everyone who values you both professionally and personally." When feeling down, Julia says revisit this list to revive yourself. Set goals for your transition period. Take occasional breaks from the search. If you have a full calendar of activities, it will help you to avoid this spiral downward because your job does not define you.

They only want young talent.

Use your experience to your advantage. Target smaller organizations that value the experience and breadth of your skillsets. With maturity comes, superior problem-solving skills. Highlight these during interviews. Help employers to shift from "over qualified" to "great resource for the company" or "no training required" or "can mentor and lead others" or "you can make me look good."

Remember, keep a youthful outlook, a contemporary attitude is as important as experience, so continue to learn, take classes, read, talk with others about trends in the workplace and of course dress for success in 20XX not 1990.

I have applied to so many companies on-line and don't even hear crickets.

"The computer does not give you a job," she says. Julia encourages people to use online information sources to find opportunities, but stresses that you should find people at those organizations to help get you connected on the inside. (LinkedIn!) Spend no more than a few hours a day for on-line opportunities and research. Most of your search day should be spent networking, volunteering, and connecting with former colleagues and employed friends. A personal reference trumps all others.

It is so hard to stay motivated.

Make a schedule – just like you had when you were employed. A structured day is powerful. Include social, personal and job search activities. Get involved with volunteer organizations to keep you connected. "The HBA kept me engaged with my industry and other professionals," says Julia. "Volunteering kept me in contact with potential employers and friends. It gave my day structure and created balance with the job search. I used my volunteer roles to develop new skills that enhanced my resume."

I hate socializing ... and telling people I am unemployed.

Social-Netting™ is a critical part of your job search. This is no time to sit at home eating (cheap) bonbons. People can't help you if they do not know you need help.

People see your human side during social events and they get to know you, which can open doors. Don't dwell on your unemployed status during these interactions or people will avoid you. Socializing relieves the job search stress and offers you chances to make contacts. "I made a connection at a wine tasting," says Julia. "It ultimately led to my new position."

I will have to take a pay cut.

Know your financial requirements before you go to market. Maybe you'll take a cut in pay, but remember you should negotiate on the things that matter most; for instance, less pay and a shorter commute = better quality of life or less pay plus a car = comparable value; less pay, but stock options = more value. Getting your foot in the door may mean a better opportunity with a company as you help it grow and thrive.

MARY LASSITER

Digital Technology and Social Media Marketing Expert, Entrepreneur

Career transition has an international twist for some people.

Moving family and career across oceans and continents presents its own set of complexities. For Mary Lassiter, it was a move from Seattle to France... Ooh, la, la!

In 2006, Mary Lassiter was working for Microsoft in Seattle when her employer offered her a temporary assignment in the South of France. Her boyfriend (now husband), Mike had been a Francophile since he was a child, so he was delighted, when Mary asked him to come along.

Mary was in charge of logistics between two companies collaborating on a tech event. "It was my first time working abroad and I had no idea what to expect. I asked Mike to join me as a translator. He had studied French for eight years which made him fluent, in my view."

The experience was so great for both Mary and Michael that they decided to move to France. In 2007 they began a five-year adventure, living first in Paris and later bought a house in Chantilly.

Jobs secured, settling into life as ex-patriots went smoothly.

After a few years, they settled into their new lives and were now fluent in French. Mary was working as a marketing consultant and Mike as an engineering consultant. Both are avid athletes and participated in bike rides across Europe and running and swimming events.

Loss of a key client translated to a search for new employment.

All was well until the company Mary worked for lost a major client. Then the company simply stopped paying its consultants. After two months without a paycheck and an unaccountable employer, she began searching for another job.

Mike's company treated its consultants similarly. This made his low-by-American standards salary less palatable. Soon they were both seeking new jobs. However, the European economy was now in a downturn and unemployment and job opportunities in France and beyond were nowhere to be found.

Time to consider another bold move.

After an unsatisfying search across the European continent for alternative employment, Mary and Mike left France and returned to the United States. Mary was disappointed, nervous and tired all of the time.

A professional network extends support across the Atlantic.

In May of 2012, the couple flew to the U.S. and began networking and scouting for jobs. Mary realized success would come through using every sales tactic possible. In addition to joining groups through LinkedIn, Mary began "cold calling" companies. One of her new LinkedIn connections was Cindy Glass, a member of the WIT network. When Mary was in the U.S., they met for coffee; Cindy told her about WIT.

Because WIT had no web presence, she was unable to learn very much about the group prior to attending a meeting. Mary went to her first meeting not knowing what to expect. She discovered a room full of women in transition just like her. She passed around business cards and met members during her U.S. visit. It wasn't long before Mary was flooded with emails of encouragement from WIT members. Even the simple emails helped her make it through the months ahead.

Edgy, risk-taking = creativity.

Many people prefer not to be edgy, risk-takers; however, sometimes what appears to be risk-taking is actually a creative response to adversity. When in a new environment, creative tactics can ease immersion and acceptance.

During her extended visit to the U.S., Mary seized the opportunity to schedule meetings with several prospective employers. Having researched each employer prior to the meetings, she responded to rejections by offering to facilitate business-to-business connections. In a short period of time, she was able to successfully complete a deal and acquire a lucrative finder's fee for her efforts.

Through cold-calls and coffee klatches, she gained valuable insights about herself. She learned she could make smart business decisions and people were interested in her experience in France. Most importantly, she was able to use those insights to differentiate herself in job search.

In June 2012, Mary and Mike returned to France and prepared to move back to the United States. Both were apprehensive since they would be returning to the U.S. without employment. To add to an already stressful situation, the process of coordinating an international relocation, without professional help, was extremely challenging. Mary found the support of family and new connections reassured her decision and helped her feel optimistic about finding a job.

By September 2012, they were back in the U.S. - permanently with just seven suitcases. She immediately put on her business attire and started networking. She reconnected with her contacts and did "net-walking" (networking while walking) sessions with WIT women.

Scenario planning early in career transition.

It helps to do scenario planning early in career transition. In addition to primary job search plan, make a plan for alternate scenarios such as, a new job that requires relocation or a spouse losing his

/her job while you are in a job search. This allows you to rapidly engage a plan as circumstances change; thus, reducing the stress and strain.

While job searching, Mary worked on creating a clothing line. One of her contacts learned of this entrepreneurial pursuit and connected her with the Women's Business Forum (WBF) of Bucks County, PA.

Through WBF, Mary connected with a mentor who helped her navigate the clothing industry. Mary's mentor founded her own clothing company as a single mom. The company eventually grew to become a multi-million dollar success.

By the end of October 2012, her tenacious networking yielded two solid job offers. She enjoyed having companies compete for her! In addition, her clothing line was coming together well. In November Mary accepted a job with a local interactive digital marketing company. The position matched her skills nicely and the opportunity seemed promising.

Keep in mind that the job you land may not last so keep your network alive.

Shortly after joining the company, business slumped and it no longer offered the opportunity Mary needed, so she pursued another job. A few months later, she interviewed with a healthcare technology company based in New York City. In a matter of weeks, she accepted their offer and now works from home with occasional travel to New York.

The transition process helped Mary build her self-confidence. The risks she took revealed her strengths and increased her self-awareness. She learned how to manage ambiguous situations and, as an entrepreneur she learned to become comfortable with uncertainty because she knows it can lead to success.

Photo: Mary Lassiter with her husband, Michael, visit the Statue of Liberty.

JUDY LOHR
Human Resources Information System Manager, SPHR*

Judy Lohr, Human Resources professional, with experience in Human Resources Information System Management (HRIS), Systems Training, and Benefits Management, was in transition twice within 17 months.

Her first transition came after years of service at Wyeth. An acquisition of Wyeth by Pfizer resulted in a workforce reduction impacting Judy. When the job she had landed following the organizational change did not work out, she decided not to rush into the next job.

Judy refers to her former colleagues at Wyeth as family. She felt at home there and had a strong sense of security. It was this bond that made the change feel so much worse. Of course, Judy was far from alone. The pharmaceutical industry was in contraction and many others also felt the impact.

Judy found it disheartening to find so many smart, capable, talented people struggling to find work. This also meant unprecedented competition for the few available jobs.

Making a plan and sticking to it is important.

During the initial transition, Judy went into an information-gathering mode and quickly became a regular at the outplacement center. She took classes on resume writing, interviewing and social media for the job search. Her goal was to land a job.

Thanks to a good severance package and transition resources which included company paid outplacement and WIT, Judy felt empowered and confident about the path to her next role. She made a plan and landed a job in 12 months.

Don't rush to accept an offer.

Judy researched the job market and prepared herself for the interview process during her first job search. She accepted a job offer based upon the positive rapport she had with a hiring manager and the manager's vision for restructuring the company, which was compatible with Judy's skillset and experience.

The hiring manager departed shortly after Judy joined the company. Judy realized the broader organization was not aligned with her former manager's vision. In four months, Judy found herself in transition again. This time she did not have a severance package or outplacement. Judy realized she should have researched the company more before accepting the offer.

With new focus, she identified and researched target companies. She had two major, non-pharmaceutical dream companies: Disney ("the most magical place on earth") and QVC (home shopping network). Ultimately, the second transition search paid off and Judy landed an HR Analyst role with QVC, a fantastic opportunity for which she is grateful and excited. The new position proved to be a great fit and shortly after starting, Judy was promoted to Manager HR Services.

Seize the opportunity for knowledge exchange.

Offer your skills to help others and it's likely they will reciprocate. For Judy, this exchange helped her use social media to showcase her knowledge. Judy used her HR knowledge and experience to help others and accepted help from others.

To start, Judy became a guest blogger for an HR professional website and joined Twitter to tweet tips for job hunters. It helped broaden her network in an important career channel. Assisting other job hunters brought Judy unexpected and extraordinary benefits. She felt empowered and regained confidence.

Strengths may be discovered and reinforced through the feedback of others.

Like many people, Judy was better acquainted with her faults than her strengths. However, the more she made herself accessible to others via social media and networking, senior industry leaders were increasingly reaching out to her for advice. Her HR experience and what she learned through outplacement equipped her with the know-how to assist others. By helping others, she discovered new strengths and more confidence in her value.

Job Search: Structure and discipline makes the process more efficient and productive. But, include down time for activities that are fun and energizing.

During her second transition, Judy realized the importance of structure. She attended regular networking meetings and even became a co-chair for one organization. She assumed an informal leadership role in an HR group, and regularly attended HR professional meetings at the Great Valley Forge Human Resources Association and the Chester County Human Resources Association.

Judy adhered to a "5-5-5" rule which required her to send five emails, make five calls, and to have five face-to-face meetings each week. This process expanded her network and increased the opportunity for productive leads and outcomes. In addition, Judy aimed for three high-value activities (HVAs) each day.

For relaxation and balance, she intentionally planned time to attend art exhibits and lectures. She was even able to get in a trip Disney with her husband. Living life in balance gave her more energy and increased her productivity.

She loves her new job and hopes to be with her company for a long time.

MARYA MARGOLIS
Pharm. D., Medical Science Liaison

It helps to be well-educated and highly specialized. However, job loss can happen to anyone.

Because Marya is highly educated and her area of expertise is specialized, she considered herself immune to job loss. When transition became a reality - not just once, but three times - it challenged her self-confidence.

After her first downsizing from a large pharma corporation in 2006, she found employment quickly with a smaller company focused on women's health products. By 2008 the new company was purchased by a large global company. In 2010, despite surviving two years of company consolidations and downsizing, her position was eliminated.

Even after a second downsizing, Marya was optimistic based on her past experience - she expected this job search process to produce similar rapid results.

Job search success sometimes requires an action plan change.

When the next job didn't come as fast, she used transition as a learning and development opportunity. For most of her career, she thought of her highly specialized skillset as a perfect fit within major pharmaceutical companies and their medical affairs groups. Therefore her view of potential employers had been singularly focused on those companies.

While being out of work is scary and uncomfortable, it can also be time for self-discovery. New and stronger relationships, as well as personal insights, can be realized during transition.

She began to think about different options, which ultimately broadened her job search scope. This expanded view prompted her to research opportunities for which she could apply her skills to roles within a variety of functional areas beyond medical affairs groups.

Her expanded target company list included a range of organizations that offered support services to large manufacturers. Additionally, she considered positions where travel was required. These adjustments landed her a new position at a medical affairs company, which provides outsourced services to pharmaceutical, biotech, and medical device companies. And the position matched her revised career objectives.

These days, job change and transition are commonplace.

Planning for serial employment is a good idea because it offers benefits for those who seize the opportunities. Perhaps most notable is liberation from "golden handcuffs" which historically kept many dissatisfied workers from moving onto more satisfying work. In today's employment climate, there is greater freedom to move if the workplace does not meet your needs.

Marya's employer, an outsourced resource, is dependent upon client companies for business. When client companies cut costs or restructure, there are likely to be immediate effects for the vendor company. She experienced these effects and was downsized for a third time. During her most recent transition, she took a long-awaited trip to Italy with her husband. This transition turned out to be brief. Marya landed back at the same employer within a short time.

Marya's Challenges:

- Marketplace challenges can be stressful when you are close to retirement
- Sometimes apparent nearness to retirement can signal a negative for an employer

Marya's Tips

- Make nearness to retirement work to your advantage
- She branded herself as flexible, experienced, knowledgeable, and as an employee who requires minimal management and who can "hit the ground running."

EILEEN O'BRIEN
Social Media Opinion Leader

Trust your instincts.

In 2009, Eileen saw the "writing on the wall." She had been leading a search, analytics and social media team at an agency but had a feeling business wasn't doing well. When she raised the issue with her boss she was reassured that everything was fine. Six weeks later, she and several others at the agency suddenly lost their jobs.

She was unemployed without the benefit of severance or support services such as outplacement. Even having the advantage of her in-demand digital media experience, it took Eileen six months to find her next employment opportunity.

Virtual network strategy yields rapid results and long-term benefits.

As you might expect, Eileen's network - which she cultivated over two years - was virtual. Despite not being a member of traditional professional organizations, her virtual one, particularly Twitter, was highly valuable. She posted she was seeking a job and her virtual network connected her to leads that progressed to interviews. Two weeks later, she was offered a job, but declined because it wasn't the right fit.

During her search, Eileen continued via her Twitter network to follow and comment on pharma industry trends. She also reached out and asked to guest blog on a few sites. It was this vibrant community of Twitter exchanges that engaged Frieda Hernandez, Vice President of Strategic Initiatives for Siren Interactive (a Chicago-based Relationship Marketing Experts for Rare Disease Disorders), who reached out to Eileen. When Frieda learned Eileen was looking for a job, they met for coffee the next time Frieda was in Philadelphia.

Over coffee, Frieda told Eileen she had been following her on Twitter for a while. She was impressed with Eileen's social media expertise and its application in healthcare, especially rare diseases. Frieda shared her company was focused in the rare disease space and felt Eileen would be a good fit. Frieda offered Eileen a position, which Eileen accepted.

For a while, Eileen hosted her own Tweetchat, #socpharm, where she led weekly chats. Eileen continues to be active online with Facebook, Twitter, and blogging.

Virtual Networking creates connection.

"I like Twitter," says Eileen, "because, the 140 character limit allows for concise communication." She makes great, high value connections through social media to reach like-minded people. "I read *"The Forever Fix: Gene Therapy and the Boy Who Saved It."* I later reached out to the author, Ricki Lewis, via Twitter and when she was in town I got to meet her over coffee."

Use social media to bolster your professional presence.

If you use social media effectively, employment recruiters are likely to be among those who follow you. Eileen recommends women in search of professional opportunities develop a personal brand. With social media resources, such as guest blogging, Facebook, Pinterest, Instagram, Twitter, and LinkedIn literally at your fingertips, a person in job search mode can readily draw attention to their knowledge, skills and career interests.

"When you meet someone and connect via LinkedIn afterward, let them know in a note where you met and perhaps some information you recall from your conversation," says Eileen. She encourages those in transition to reach out to people via Twitter and build relationships based on areas of mutual interest. In her case a Twitter contact led to a job opportunity. Of course, the human factor is still very important. Virtual connectivity should not replace face-to-face interaction.

"My job search was about self-awareness. The six-month search was longer than I hoped, but it gave me an opportunity to evaluate what was important," says Eileen.

When the corporate office and your home are in different cities, you adapt.

Jobs matching Eileen's unique skill sets are often nationwide as opposed to concentrated in one geographical area. She's worked for firms based in Boston, Chicago, Princeton, and NYC, while living in Philadelphia. Eileen worked from home and or used co-working locations such as Indy Hall or Benjamin's Desk combined with regular travel to company corporate offices and client offices.

Her adaptability opened the door to opportunities aligned with her expertise and goals.

Eileen's experience and choices provided her options that advanced her career trajectory. Resulting in her most recent role with a New York City based firm, which combines PR, social media, ad agency services and digital shop expertise to provide integrated solutions for clients.

Http://twitter.com/Eileenobrien
Http://LinkedIn.com/in/eileenobrien

SUE PRICE, MBA
Career / Executive Business Coach, Project Management Professional

For many people, career change means a transition from corporate professional to entrepreneur.

Sue Price had been with her large pharmaceutical employer a long time. An accomplished and proven professional with two graduate degrees and 30 years of pharmaceutical supply-chain management experience, Sue enjoyed corporate success until her job was eliminated. She explored several options, including the non-profit sector, starting her own career coaching business, volunteering, consulting, and a full-time contract research organization (CRO) position.

Exploring different options can be informative and rewarding.

Early in her transition, Sue accepted a position in a non-profit organization. In time the lower non-profit salary created financial pressure for her so she formed a company called Career Coach LLC. She learned so much through her own transition she discovered she could market her expertise.

Through her company, Sue offers career-coaching services to clients (which satisfies her desire to help others)_and earns the additional income needed to sustain her lifestyle. Because coaching has become a passion, she views it as a long-term full-time option that she intends to build over time.

Supporting women in career transition.

Shortly after Sue formed Career Coach, LLC, a former colleague invited Sue to visit the WIT group. The group's focus was to have speakers who could share useful information and tips to help with job searches, which sometimes involved career change.

At one of the meetings she attended, Sue was asked to present her job search strategies, which was well-received. Sue felt valued and later became co-chair of WIT.

Networking has near-term and long-term benefits.

Sue met a recruiter for the CRO role a year prior to being offered a position. She shared her professional experience with the recruiter who was impressed with her credentials but had no matches.

Eventually, the recruiter reached out to her about a full-time job working on-site for a major pharmaceutical client to help with clinical trials. Despite not having the specific experience required for the role, the recruiter saw how her skills were easily transferrable.

Volunteering creates value for everyone involved.

Giving back and serving others is important to Sue. She volunteers at the Women's Resource Center (WRC), A non-profit whose mission is to support women, strengthen families and build community through informational, referral, counseling, legal and educational services.

The WRC provided Sue with an outlet for networking and kept her busy with meaningful work during transition.

Flexibility through change will help you to flourish.

Sue enjoyed her roles as WIT Co-Chair, Consultant, CRO senior project manager, part-time career coach, and volunteer at WRC – connecting women to resources in transition.

At this writing, Sue was downsized from the CRO role due to budget cuts, but her experiences have taught her to be flexible and creative. Through networking, she pieced together income sources by connecting with two established businesses (a women's health and wellness practice and an international career coaching service company) to offer her career service expertise part-time while she continues to grow her private coaching practice. She is steadfastly working on her career coaching business but may work as a pharmaceutical consultant to balance her income as she grows her coaching practice.

DEB SWARTZ, JD
General Counsel, Chief Compliance Officer

Career transition has two tracks.

Since she was 10, Debbie Swartz knew what she wanted to be – a lawyer. She was an eager student, always raising her hand to answer questions and she loved to debate. In college she went to law school to become a litigator. Initially, she practiced law at a large firm but later moved to a small firm, just like she envisioned. Though, she eventually landed a position as associate general counsel and chief compliance officer for a global pharmaceutical distributor.

When she found herself in transition, she made the most of it. She split her time between an active job search and quality family time. She's always been committed to travel and sightseeing, so she used her schedule flexibility for monthly trips with her children, one such visit was the Titanic museum in

Tennessee. The extended time with her children was priceless. She treasured the ordinary day-to-day routines and the extraordinary experiences when traveling.

Though all transitions in life have their moments of frustration and doubt, Debbie's had a contagious optimism and positive energy that helped her through the lull periods and uplifted those around her.

High energy, high productivity, big gains

Networking wasn't a priority while Debbie was employed – her schedule didn't permit it -but when in transition, she applied the same high energy she had on the job to her networking and made big gains – going from 150 LinkedIn Connections to more than 700 people.

She likes networking, meeting new people, and helping others by facilitating introductions among her connections. She's active in a variety of professional groups, including HBA WIT and Greater Philadelphia Senior Executives Group (GPSEG).

Not all networking organizations are the same.

Learn about the networking groups in your area to determine which ones match your professional goals and personal values. Debbie discovered the HBA WIT through one of her networking connections and became a regular at meetings. WIT's members were from the same industry and included virtually every major company within that industry, an attribute she found valuable.

In a very real sense, the spirit and encouragement of the participants extended beyond the meetings. They exchanged job leads and job search resources, celebrated successes and helped overcome hurdles.

Self-awareness and sharp focus lead to establishing clear goals and that are achievable.

With a solid record of achievements and a high-powered job, Debbie expected a more favorable job market. Like many before her, she learned there were fewer available roles at her professional level.

Debbie's search led to choices concerning location and which industries she wanted. She debated whether to open up to a larger geographic area to reach more opportunities but wanted to limit disruption to her family—so she opted to stay local. She preferred in-house corporate counsel roles because she loves being a part of a team and likes to help develop highly productive, strong teams.

Her priorities established, she charted a course based on local opportunities and expanded her search to other industries. Ultimately, she accepted a position close to home as Vice President of Legal Affairs and Chief Compliance Officer for a graduate education financial non-profit membership organization. Her role encompasses legal, internal audit and compliance responsibilities.

Debbie is well connected and respected lawyer, who speaks regularly on a variety of legal and compliance topics, including records and information management, e-discovery and social media.

Debbie knows that change may come again—but believes her valuable transition experiences will help her navigate them successfully.

Photo: Deb Swartz and her family
enjoying a vacation in Costa Rica.

CONCLUSION

We hope you've enjoyed the career transition journeys shared. It's likely that one or two resonated with you and where you are in your own career journey. The women who founded WIT, the women who lead it today and the women who have participated in this book provide a legacy for others through their wisdom and leadership.

ABOUT THE AUTHORS

LINDA LOJEWSKI

Award-Winning Marketer, Ventures (and Adventures!) Connector and Catalyst, founder of the Business Strategy Consulting Company, LMEL Group

As a long-time member of the Healthcare Businesswomen's Association (HBA), I was eager to support HBA's affinity group, WIT. WIT operates independently with its own leadership, structure and mission. After a few months of attending meetings, I became fascinated by how well the

WIT organization functioned through continuous flux.

Faces of leadership changed, yet the group's mission progressed without disruption. I thought WIT had a story worth telling. Subsequently, I spoke with former WIT co-chair, MaryAnne Sarzynski, who expressed her intentions to write about this unique group. And we agreed to collaborate. We shared the book idea with HBA Board members and the process began.

We kicked things off with a series of interviews intended to collect WIT facts, history and evolution, but realized these women's stories during career transition were most compelling.

I first engaged with WIT during my career transition. With more than 25 years in the pharmaceutical industry (marketing communications and public affairs at Merck, U.S. and global product marketing, payer access marketing and alliance management at Wyeth, and commercial development for biologics at Pfizer), I arrived at transition with a sense of gratitude. These companies had provided a platform for me to serve worldwide healthcare in roles that "played to my strengths."

With transition, I appreciated the opportunity that change brings. Unlike so many others, I did not have children or a spouse's career to consider. I could plan to intentionally stretch in directions that would extend outside my comfort zones. I looked forward to the growth and even the growing pains. I knew the process would help me to apply my strengths to new opportunities.

To start, I wrote a life plan based on a personal vision statement. From the vision statement, I derived five segments for focus. I then defined goals for each segment. Just as in the traditional workplace, I held myself accountable for achievement of my goals by developing sets of measurable actions. I defined metrics that indicated goal progress. In this way, I could make adjustments as needed. This approach kept me focused, disciplined and achieving my goals.

I was a WIT-co-chair for a bit more than a year. During that time, I initiated Think Tanks, a brainchild that emerged at a meeting while listening to a member remark about how much she missed using her skills. At the same time, I knew there were budget-strapped young companies who could benefit from the talent in WIT.

I formed Think Tanks as consulting panels with various participants depending on the business questions of the small company. The idea was well received among members and the companies.

With more than 100 group members representing major pharmas, management levels, and functional areas, WIT had a deep bench. I was committed to delivering high-quality results to serve both the businesses and WIT members. I knew that satisfied businesspersons would be willing to provide participants with LinkedIn recommendations and useful leads. To assure effective panels, I become familiar with the skills and experience of WIT members.

Because I had been a proactive advocate for WIT and the Think Tanks, businesses began to reach out to me, not only for Think Tanks, but for talent. Knowing WIT members well meant I was able to frequently make prospective employer/employee connections. I am very pleased to have made connections that have helped several people land jobs and helped several companies to acquire excellent employees. The Think Tanks served more than a half dozen companies during my tenure, and they continued beyond my leadership window.

It is my hope that the stories presented here will inspire and encourage those who read them.

If you would like to connect with me, please do so through LinkedIn.

Photo: Linda kayaking in LaPaz, Mexico.

Photo: Linda with husband, Bill, in Alaska.

MARYANNE SARZYNSKI

Inventive Business Solutions (Research, Strategy, Design, Implementation); Project/Program/Process Management; Principal, Ideation Spring Consulting

As an employee at a major biotech/pharma company, I was called to the cafeteria to hear news from management about a rumored "right sizing." The economy was slumping due to the recession and we were told there would be workforce changes to reduce and/or eliminate redundancy. Later that day, I found out my position was on the elimination list.

Colleague camaraderie was amazing, as I worked to finalize and/or pass along my responsibilities and projects. Management was flexible as the displaced employees sought new employment. I was given a severance package with health benefits and pay extending several months. Outplacement services were included and I began the process of learning tips for resume creation, business cards, target companies, personal bios, networking, accessing job listings electronically, and other transition information.

To stay current I invested time in enhancing my credentials: I completed the Project Management Professional (PMP) certification; the Pharmaceutical and Medical Device Law and Compliance certificate from Seton Hall Law School; attended the Small Business Development Center (SBDC) Program for Entrepreneurs at Wharton; and took several Coursera classes focused on public health, food (the economics of and as medicine), and clinical trials.

Expanding and honing my skills and increasing my network have given me some of the most rewarding times of my life professionally and personally. I have made real connections, some developing into friendships. I am grateful for meeting so many talented women and men for exchange of ideas and resource sharing.

Not long after I was introduced to WIT group during transition, I volunteered as a co-chair, which meant arranging and facilitating meetings, engaging speakers, introducing new members, and connecting members for career opportunities. I also partnered with another WIT member to develop and implement a process and centralized repository for information sharing to optimize member benefits. This work allowed me to give back as I broadened my network.

With the business and employment environment in flux, I branched out in new directions. I spent time consulting, co-authoring this e-book, exploring entrepreneurial opportunities and volunteering (to develop and deliver a pilot program for teens in transition consisting of cooking classes designed to promote collaboration, food education, nutrition, healthy eating and food economics to create happier, healthier people and communities).

Learning and exchange of ideas, and collaboration have always been a passion for me. This recent segment of my life's journey encouraged exploration in life and career, for this I am grateful. I am confident and optimistic about my future and that of the many talented people I have encountered.

Photo: MaryAnne Mountain
Climbing in The Adirondacks

DEMOGRAPHICS AND FACTS ABOUT WIT

eBook Contributors	Total	WIT	Non-WIT
Total Contributors to eBook	22	15	7
Sole or Major Providers for Household	20	14	6
Experienced Job Transition Since 2008	21	15	6
More Than One Job Transition Since 2008	9	8	1
Decade or More of Employment within Big Pharmas	14	12	2
Contracting and/or Consulting Employment Since 2008	15	9	6
Self-Employed / Starting a Business	10	6	4
Graduate and Post-Graduate Degrees	15	13	2
White / Non-White Contributors	17 / 5	13 / 2	4 / 3
> 35 years of age	21	14	7
Those Eligible for Retirement Who Are Planning to Stop Working	0	0	0
Eligible for Retirement	3	1	2

APPENDIX

WIT Job Search Resources List

Books:
- *Company Confidential: 50 Secrets Your Company Doesn't Want You to Know, and What to Do About Them* by Cynthia Shapiro
- *Finding Your North Star* by Martha Beck
- *First, Break All the Rules: What the World's Greatest Managers Do Differently* by Marcus Buckingham
- *How to Negotiate a Killer Job Offer* by Robin F Bond, Esq
- *Job Searching with Social Media for Dummies* by Joshua Waldman
- *Knock'em Dead Resumes* by Martin Yale
- *Nice Girls Don't Get the Corner Office* by Lois Frankel
- *Shut Up and Say Something* by Karen Friedman
- *Steering by Starlight* by Martha Beck
- *The Book of Lists* published by the Philadelphia Business Journal

- *The Ultimate Job Search* by Martin Yale
- *Unlock the Hidden Job Market* by Duncan Mathison and Martha Finney
- *What Does Somebody Have to Do to Get A Job Around Here? 44 Insider Secrets That Will Get You Hired* by Cynthia Shapiro

Consulting Organizations:
- A-connect (short term) www.a-connect.com
- BTG–IT Consulting (short term) www.btginc.com
- Endeavor Group http://www.endeavorcg.com
- FlexPro Group http://www.theflexprogroup.com
- Gerson Lehrman Group – register to be a consultant www.glgresearch.com
- Oxford International http://www.oxfordcorp.com
- High Point Solutions http://www.highpoint-solutions.com
- Smart Consulting (Denise Smart), http://www.smartconsultinggroup.com
- The Experts Bench http://www.tebww.com/
- Your Encore (short term) www.yourencore.com

Free Business Cards:
- Vista Print www.vistaprint.com
- Moo printing http://us.moo.com/

Local Organizations for Networking:
- ChemPharmas, http://www.chemPharmas.net/
- HBA Greater Philly Chapter, http://www.hbanet.org/chapters/greaterphilly
- HBA Metro Chapter, https://www.hbanet.org/chapters/metro

- Greater Philadelphia Executive Networking Group (GPSEG) http://www.gpseg.org/Home.aspx
- Greater Valley Forge Human Resources Association www.gvfhra.org
- LinkedIn Groups
- NJ BioPharmas Networking Group (NJBPNG)
- PA BioPharmas Networking Group (PABPNG)
- NJ Bio http://www.bionj.org/
- My Career Transitions, Penn State Great Valley http://mycareertransitions.com/new/
- Pennsylvania Bio www.pabio.org
- Pharmas Marketing Meetings http://www.meetings.Pharmas-mkting.com
- Women's Resource Center www.womensresourcecenter.com

Online Tools:

- www.wordles.net for checking resumes' keyword strength
- Reach 360, free tool for personal branding http://www.reachcc.com/360reach
- Linked In www.linkedin.com
- Linked In training Greig Wells, www.BeFoundJobs.com, www.JobSearchSmarter.com
- http://pinkmirror.com, free site offers photo retouching to help you look your best
- www.Startwire.com, site that tracks and alerts you as your on-line application moves through the hiring process for companies that use the common applications such as Taleo

Job Search Websites:
- www.biospace.com has jobs, company information and career fairs
- www.indeed.com
- http://jobcircle.com/
- http://www.bionjtalentnetwork.org

Personal Branding:
- Cecilia Stoeckicht, http://www.imageatelier.com/about.html
- Lori Tevis, co-owner and executive stylist for Worth, https://www.worthnewyork.com/

Entrepreneur Opportunities/Forums:
- Entrepreneur's Forum of Greater Philadelphia http://www.efgp.org
- Enterpreneur Works of Greater Philadelphia http://www.myentrepreneurworks.org/about
- UpStart University of Pennsylvania (Center for Technology Transfer) http://www.ctt.upenn.edu/upstart.html
- Bio Advance (Life Science Start Up Funding) http://www.bioadvance.com
- Women's Business Forum http://www.womens businessforum.org

Employment Law:
- Kimberly H. Ashback, Esq http://www.ashbachlaw.com
- Robin Bond, Esq (Founder of Transition Strategies LLC) http://www.transition-strategies
- Sidney Gold & Associates, P.C. Philadelphia, http://www.discrimlaw.net/

Salary and Corporation Profile Information:
- www.salary.com
- www.simplyhired.com
- www.manta.com
- www.glassdoor.com

State Benefits and Resources:
- Pennsylvania Career Links: Pennsylvania Workforce Development
- http://www.paworkforce.state.pa.us/portal/server.pt/community/pa_workforce_development/12865
    - Monetary Grants available for retraining course/certifications
    (Includes PMP-Project Management Professional)
    - Grant amounts are county specific (Montgomery, Bucks, Chester, Delaware, etc.)
    - Attend in person orientation to qualify at unemployment office
    - Skill test may be required to qualify: Math, Reading, Finding Information

Career Coaches:
- Matt Levy Corner Office career coaching http://www.cornerofficecoach.com/services.html
- Linda DeLuca (Executive *Coach, Presentation Skills*) http://azione-scopo.com http://meet.lindadeluca.com
- Alex Freund, www.landingexpert.com
- Kelleher and Associates LLC. (*Career and Executive Coaching*) http://www.kelleherllc.com

- Abby Kohut, speaker and career coach www.absolutelyabby.com\
- Mary O'Connor Apollo Leadership Capital, LLC.
- Safiya Edwards, Career and Coaching, www.linkedin.com/in/safiya

Affordable Health Insurance:
- https://www.ehealthinsurance.com
- http://www.singlesrising.com/affordablehealth insurance.html

Free Credit Score:
- www.CreditKarma.com

Recruiters, Search Consultants:
- Ruderfer & Associates, Inc (www.ruderfer.com) – Steve Bass, PhD stevenbassra@me.com and Irwin Ruderfer irwin@ruderfer.com
- Shellie Caplan, at Caplan Associates, http://www.caplanassoc.com

Courses and Certifications:
- Project Management Professional (PMP) Certification
  - Project Management Institute (PMI) http://www.pmi.org/Certification/Project-Management-Professional-PMP.aspx
  - PMP Education Credits for Exam and CEUs from PM Podcast (self-paced modules) http://www.project-management-podcast.com

- Free University Courses (MOOCs—Massive Open Online Courses). Generally, non-credit but can earn certificates via completion of assignments. Broad subject range from HealthCare to Business offered by Johns Hopkins, University of Pennsylvania, Duke, Princeton, University of California and many others.

    https://www.coursera.org
    https://www.udemy.com